W9-BDW-307

REAL REVOLUTIONARIES

THE REAL
AARON
BURR

THE TRUTH BEHIND THE LEGEND

by Eric Braun

Content Consultant:
Richard Bell
Associate Professor of History
University of Maryland, College Park

COMPASS POINT BOOKS
a capstone imprint

Real Revolutionaries is published by Compass Point Books,
1710 Roe Crest Drive, North Mankato, Minnesota 56003
www.capstonepub.com

Library of Congress Cataloging-in-Publication Data is available on the Library of Congress website.
Names: Braun, Eric, 1971– author.
Title: The Real Aaron Burr : The Truth Behind the Legend / by Eric Braun.
Description: North Mankato, Minn. : Capstone Press, 2019. | Series: Real Revolutionaries |
Includes bibliographical references and index. | Audience: Grades 7–8. | Audience: Age 13.
Identifiers: LCCN 2019014610 (print) | LCCN 2019016109 (ebook) | ISBN 9780756562540
(eBook PDF) | ISBN 9780756562502 (library binding)
Subjects: LCSH: Burr, Aaron, 1756–1836—Juvenile literature. | Vice-Presidents—United
States—Biography—Juvenile literature. | Burr-Hamilton Duel, Weehawken, N.J., 1804—
Juvenile literature. | Soldiers—United States—Biography—Juvenile literature. | United States—
History—Revolution, 1775–1783—Biography—Juvenile literature.
Classification: LCC E302.6.B9 (ebook) | LCC E302.6.B9 B74 2019 (print) |
DDC 973.4/6092 [B]—dc23
LC record available at https://lccn.loc.gov/2019014610

Editorial Credits
Mandy Robbins, editor; Sarah Bennett, designer; Eric Gohl, media researcher; Kathy McColley, production specialist

Photo Credits
Alamy: Art Collection 2, 13, Everett Collection Inc, 17, History and Art Collection, 20, 39, Niday Picture Library, 43, Old Paper Studios, 19, Pictures Now, 57; Getty Images: Bettmann, 34, 50, The New York Historical Society, 49; Granger: 29; Library of Congress: 10; North Wind Picture Archives: 7, 25, 33; Wikimedia: Public Domain, cover, 1, 8, 14, 22, 26, 36, 45, Tony, 54

Design Elements
Shutterstock

Printed and bound in the USA
PA71

Contents

CHAPTER ONE

ACCOMPLISHED FOUNDING FATHER

For much of U.S. history, Aaron Burr has been considered a villain for killing Alexander Hamilton. But Burr played a key role in forming the new country. He fought bravely in the Revolutionary War (1775–1783). In fact, he never stopped fighting for what he thought was right and fair, even when it angered other powerful leaders. That—and the fact that his enemies were so successful in bad-mouthing him—may be why he is one of the most disliked of the founding fathers.

REVOLUTIONARY WAR HERO

At just 19 years old, Burr was an unlikely war hero. He was the grandson of a famous scholar and the son of a university president. It seemed likely that he would grow up to be an academic like them.

Both of Burr's parents died before he turned three, so he went to live with an uncle. There he was able to focus on his studies from a young age. Burr entered Princeton University at just 13 years old. He graduated at age 16. By 1775, he was studying law. The first battles of the American Revolution began that year. Nineteen-year-old Burr took a break from his studies to join the cause.

He volunteered to join a mission to attack the British province of Quebec in Canada. The mission was led by Colonel Benedict Arnold. Nearly 1,000 Continental Army soldiers set off from Cambridge, Massachusetts, in September 1775. But the journey took far longer than expected. When they finally reached Quebec, Arnold's troops were starving. Many had died or turned back.

Colonel Arnold's troops weren't strong enough to conquer the city. Instead, they holed up nearby to wait for reinforcements. The reinforcements were in Montreal, being led by General Richard Montgomery. Burr had impressed his commander during the difficult march. Arnold sent Burr to meet Montgomery and lead him to Quebec. Montgomery and Burr formed a strong friendship right away. They arrived at the Continental Army camp outside Quebec in early December. Burr was promoted to the rank of captain for his efforts.

For most of December, the patriot troops planned their attack on Quebec. On December 31, they attacked—and suffered a disastrous loss. Canadian militiamen were hiding in a blockhouse. They had no trouble shooting the advancing Americans, who were out in the open. Colonel Arnold was wounded, and General Montgomery was killed. The Americans retreated.

Some people who witnessed the battle said that Burr went back out into the field of battle. He risked his life under fire of the Canadians to try to recover General

John Trumbull's painting *The Death of General Montgomery in the Attack on Quebec, December 31, 1775,* shows the fatally wounded Montgomery falling into the arms of one of his men.

Montgomery's body. The stories said he lifted the larger man and brought him part of the way back. But he couldn't carry him all the way through the snow. Whether he went back for Montgomery's body or not, he did lead the troops back to safety.

Burr had shown great bravery and leadership in battle. He was rewarded by being promoted to serve on General George Washington's personal staff in New York City. But after just a few weeks on the job, Burr left. It's not known exactly why. Some people say the two did not get along. Whatever happened, Burr moved on to serve General Israel Putnam. He fought in the Battle of Long Island and helped evacuate New York City as the British took it over. In June 1777, at the age of 21, Burr became a lieutenant colonel.

RADICAL LAWYER AND STATE SENATOR

After leaving the Continental Army in 1779, Burr picked up his studies where he had left off before joining the Army. At age 26, he completed his study of law and passed the exam to become a lawyer in New York in 1782. He got married that same year, and the next year he moved to New York City to set up a law practice.

It turned out to be a lucky time to break into the field of law in New York City. For many years, most lawyers in the city had been Tories. They were people who had been loyal to the British. But after the American Revolution,

Burr (left) successfully defended Levi Weeks against the charge of murder in one of the most high-profile and dramatic court cases of the time. He claimed Richard Croucher (right) was the true murderer.

New York passed a law that banned Tories from practicing law. As a result, when Burr set up his practice, he had very little competition. He was able to get a lot of work and quickly built a reputation as a good lawyer. One client described him as someone who never gave up on a case and never shirked his responsibilities.

Many legal cases at that time involved slaves or former slaves. Burr owned slaves—as did most of his peers.

But unlike most of those peers, Burr encouraged his slaves to learn to read and write, and to study more complicated subjects. As a lawyer, he defended slave-owners' rights. But he also represented freed slaves. For instance, one of his clients was a freed slave who was suing to get his portion of an inheritance from his former owner, who was also his father.

A career in law has long been a common pathway to a career in politics. Burr soon became involved in New York's political world. In 1784, he was elected to the New York Assembly as a state senator. During his two-year term, Burr's views on slavery seemed to become more radical. He once proposed a bill calling for the immediate freeing of all slaves. He opposed a law that fined black people who married white people. And he also opposed three different amendments that restricted the rights of free blacks. One said that free blacks could not vote. One said that they could not serve on a jury. The last said that they could not testify in court against a white person. Burr also supported women's rights. In 1785, he proposed allowing women to vote, becoming one of the first Americans to do so.

During these years, Burr also developed his political viewpoint. At the time, there were two major groups of political thought. The Federalists believed in a strong central government. They wanted to approve the new Constitution of the United States. Alexander Hamilton was a prominent New York Federalist. The members of the other group were called anti-Federalists. They did not want a strong national government. They believed it would lead to too few people having too much power. Burr favored this group.

EARLY FEMINIST

In the late 1700s, the word *feminism* didn't exist. Women had few rights in the new United States. They were expected to get married and take care of a home and children. Nearly everybody accepted that women and girls were not as smart or as capable as men or boys. Families focused on their sons' education. Even in families with enough money to hire tutors or send children to school, girls were rarely educated. They might learn art or music. But they were almost never educated in more serious subjects such as math, languages, or philosophy.

Very few women talked about women's rights. Even fewer men did. So it was highly unusual that the young state senator Aaron Burr proposed a bill that would allow women to vote. The bill didn't become law—but it showed that Burr was one of the first people eager to give women full and equal rights. He also proved this in his personal life. In 1782, he married Theodosia Prevost Bartow. She was a widow who had five children and was 10 years older than Burr. She also fought for women's rights.

The Burrs had an unusual marriage for their time. In most marriages, wives were expected to obey their husbands. But the Burrs agreed that their marriage would be a marriage of equals. Aaron Burr respected his wife's mind. He once wrote that she was one of the smartest people he knew. They discussed issues such as philosophy and politics—topics that were usually discussed only between men.

A year after they married, the Burrs had a daughter. They named her Theodosia, after her mother. Both Burrs doted on their daughter. Aaron became an unusually involved father. It was common for mothers to be in

A painting thought to be of Burr's daughter, Theodosia, was discovered in 1869 in Nag's Head, North Carolina.

charge of raising children. Men focused on their careers and the outside world, while women focused on their families. But many letters between the Burrs show Aaron Burr was very involved in his daughter's upbringing.

The Burrs decided to educate their daughter as if she were a boy. They hired the best teachers they could find. Even when Burr was away serving in Congress, he sent detailed instructions for Theodosia's education. She learned Greek, French, Latin, math, and geography, as well as literature and music. Theodosia Burr was considered the most well-educated girl of her time.

Years later, Burr and his wife both came to admire the work of Mary Wollstonecraft, an English writer on

women's rights. Wollstonecraft argued that women deserved the same rights, education, and career opportunities as men. She also said that fathers should be involved in their children's upbringing. She basically stated the ideas that the Burrs used to raise their daughter.

Mary Wollstonecraft

When Burr first read Wollstonecraft's essay, *A Vindication of the Rights of Woman,* he was a U.S. senator. He called the essay a "work of genius." And he wrote to his wife about his frustrations that nobody else seemed to appreciate the value of Wollstonecraft's ideas. "Is it owing to ignorance or prejudice that I have not yet met a single person who had discovered or would allow the merit of this work?" He wrote that he felt his daughter's purpose was to prove to the world that Wollstonecraft was right and that "women have souls."

Tragically, Burr's wife died in 1794 at age 48. She had been ill for a long time, possibly with cancer. Burr was heartbroken. But he was determined to raise 10-year-old Theodosia the way he and his wife had planned. Even as a U.S. senator and vice president, he devoted himself to guiding her education. Theodosia married in 1801. She soon had a son. But she also died young—at the age of 29. She was lost at sea as she traveled by boat from her home in South Carolina to visit her father in New York.

CAMPAIGN TRAILBLAZER

Although he served as both U.S. senator and vice president, Burr's biggest contribution to American politics might have come on the campaign trail. Many people say he invented political campaigning as it exists today. There's no doubt that Burr changed the way political campaigns took place in the United States.

Burr achieved this through some simple ideas that he put into place during the 1800 presidential election. In that election, President John Adams was running for re-election against Vice President Thomas Jefferson. Adams was a member of the Federalist Party, and Jefferson was a Democratic-Republican. Burr was running to be Jefferson's vice president, also as a Democratic-Republican.

Today that election is remembered because Burr ended up tying with Jefferson to be president. That part of history is its own story. But another part of history often gets lost in the details of the tie. That's the story of how Burr invented a new twist to the idea of political campaigning. In doing so, he helped get himself and Jefferson elected.

At the time, elections were decided by members of the Electoral College. Those members were appointed by each state's legislature. In the run-up to the 1800 election, the New York Assembly included mostly Federalists. They would appoint Electoral College members who would vote for Adams. Burr knew he needed to change this in order to get votes for himself and Jefferson. He needed to add more Democratic-Republicans to the Assembly.

Burr knew that many immigrants and working-class people disliked Adams. They hated a set of laws he had passed called the Alien and Sedition Acts. These laws took away rights from immigrants. Burr knew he could gain immigrant support for the

FIFTH *CONGRESS* OF THE UNITED STATES:

At the Second Session.

Begun and held at the city of *Philadelphia*, in the ſtate of PENNSYLVANIA, on *Monday*, the thirteenth of *November*, one thouſand ſeven hundred and ninety-ſeven.

An ACT *concerning aliens.*

BE it enacted by the Senate and House of Representatives of the United States of America, in Congreſs aſſembled, *That it ſhall be lawful for the Preſident of the United States at any time during the continuance of this act, to order all such aliens as he ſhall judge dangerous to the peace and ſafety of the United States, or ſhall have reaſonable grounds to ſuſpect are concerned in any treaſonable or ſecret machinations against the government thereof, to depart out of the territory of the United States, within ſuch time as ſhall be expreſſed in ſuch order...*

The Alien and Sedition Acts tightened restrictions on immigrants and outlawed speech criticizing the government.

Democratic-Republican Party. And he knew that a lot of immigrants lived in New York City. All he had to do was get them out to vote for Democratic-Republican assemblymen. Then the Democratic-Republicans would outnumber the Federalists in the New York Assembly—and they would appoint more Electoral College members who would vote for Jefferson and Burr.

Burr came up with a plan to get more New York City immigrants to vote. He knew that many were involved in a new social club called the Society of Saint Tammany. Immigrants and other working-class New Yorkers would gather at the club to socialize. Burr didn't belong to the club, but he went and talked to members. He reminded them that the Federalists did not respect their rights. And he asked them to go door to door and convince their friends and families to vote for Democratic-Republican assemblymen. He also got them to raise money from local businesses. They used the money to help spread the word even more. And it worked. New York City elected Democratic-Republicans to the state assembly. And they, in turn, appointed Democratic-Republican supporters to the Electoral College. These men elected Jefferson and Burr over Adams.

Door-to-door campaigning soon became a standard in American elections. And the Society of Saint Tammany soon became known as Tammany Hall. Due to its influence in getting candidates elected, Tammany Hall became the most powerful political organization in

Tammany Hall played a major role in New York City politics from the 1790s to the 1960s.

New York City. For more than 150 years, it was responsible for the Democratic Party having the majority of control over New York City politics.

U.S. SENATOR AND VICE PRESIDENT

In 1794, a new painting of Senator Aaron Burr was completed. As opposed to typical portraits of politicians at the time, Burr was not wearing a wig in the painting. He was not wearing a fancy, frilly shirt or gold buttons. Instead, he looked plain, yet youthful, and full of vigor.

Gilbert Stuart's 1794 portrait of Burr broke with
the traditional style of political portraits.

Burr had taken his seat in the U.S. Senate in 1791 by
defeating Philip Schuyler, a rich and powerful landholder
who was 23 years older than him. Schuyler represented
the kind of man who had held office in the United
States since the country's founding. Unlike Schuyler,

Burr was not a member of elite society. The significance of the painting was clear. Burr represented a new kind of political power that was on the rise. He represented enlightenment. He represented energy. He represented possibilities.

Burr served on about 60 Senate committees. Topics he favored included public lands on the frontier and veterans' rights. He worked to get pensions for veterans and help those disabled by war. He also worked to help the widows and orphans of veterans. He supported increasing the size of the military on the frontier, where the U.S. Army was fighting American Indian tribes.

Burr became popular in the Democratic-Republican party and with many Federalists. He was an independent thinker who was not blindly loyal to either political party. Instead, he acted as a moderate. He didn't have ties to any of the old wealthy families who had run politics for so long. Because of this, he made decisions based on information rather than loyalty to old power.

By the time Burr's term as senator ended, he had made lots of friends in politics and established a reputation as a smart, up-and-coming political force. He served two more years in the New York assembly. In 1800, he landed a spot on the presidential ticket with prominent Democratic-Republican Thomas Jefferson. After the election ended in a tie—with John Adams coming in third—voting moved to the members of the House of Representatives to break the tie. After much political dealing, arguing, and promising, and 36 rounds of voting, Jefferson was finally voted into the presidency, with Aaron Burr as his vice president.

Thomas Jefferson

But the election tie and the wrangling that followed may have hurt Burr's career even if it landed him the vice presidency. Some people thought he had tried to cheat Jefferson out of the presidency. Others thought he appeared too weak, deferring to Jefferson. His reputation took a hit.

Within a year, Jefferson had begun to distrust Burr. He wanted his secretary of state and fellow Virginian James Madison to be the next president. But Aaron Burr would seem the natural successor to Jefferson. In 1804, after Burr killed Hamilton in a duel, Jefferson had the opportunity he was waiting for. He replaced Burr as vice president with George Clinton. Clinton was a Democratic-Republican who had been governor of New York. Burr ran for governor of New York after that, but he lost. Being vice president—and earning the distrust of Thomas Jefferson—had effectively ended his political career.

CHAPTER TWO
BURR IN MYTHS

Burr's critics were very successful in spreading negative stories about him. However, many of them are untrue. Burr certainly deserved criticism for some of his actions, but some of the negative stories were exaggerated or totally false.

RELENTLESS BULLY?

Aaron Burr is probably most well known for the duel in which he shot and killed Alexander Hamilton. For most of U.S. history, the stories behind this duel painted Burr as the bully. Burr's bullying finally reached a climax when he challenged Hamilton and murdered him. The duel on the shore of the Hudson River in New Jersey is an important story in U.S. history.

The problem with this version of history is that it's not really true. Yes, Hamilton and Burr were rivals in politics. Hamilton didn't just disagree with Burr's ideas about government. He thought Burr was dangerous for the country. Hamilton was a member of the Federalist Party, which believed in a strong central government. Burr was a Democratic-Republican. He believed power should be held more among the states. Although Hamilton felt very strongly about his party, Burr was often willing to compromise. He would work with either party to find solutions. While some may see that as a good quality, Hamilton didn't trust him because of it.

The two men's rivalry went back to the Revolutionary War, when two generals were vying for control of the Continental Army. One was George Washington, whom Hamilton favored. The other was Charles Lee, Burr's preference. In the summer of 1778, General Washington and his army pursued the British Army into New Jersey. When the British stopped to rest, Washington spoke with his advisors. Several, including Hamilton, advised attacking. Others, including Lee, suggested holding back.

Washington ordered the attack, but after the fighting started, Lee retreated. One of the officers leading the army was Aaron Burr. He saw that the battle was a disaster for the Americans. He thought Lee had done the right thing and saved many lives. But Washington was furious. When it was over, General Lee was court-martialed for disobeying orders.

In a preview of how he would later treat Burr, Hamilton spread nasty rumors and gossip about Lee. In turn, Lee compared Hamilton to a disgusting insect, calling him a "dirty earwig." Burr wrote a letter defending Lee, but it didn't help. Lee was convicted and demoted.

George Washington angrily confronted
General Charles Lee at the Battle of Monmouth.

After the war, Burr and Hamilton pursued careers in politics. Hamilton's distrust toward Burr grew in 1791. That was the year Burr won the position of U.S. Senator from New York. The man Burr defeated in that race was Philip Schuyler, Hamilton's father-in-law. This angered Hamilton. It wasn't only about

Alexander Hamilton

family loyalty. Hamilton had become the U.S. Treasury Secretary under President Washington. Hamilton and Schuyler were building a network of power in the new nation, especially in New York. Losing the spot to Burr was a blow to his political goals.

Hamilton saw Burr as a powerful opponent, and over the years he worked hard to make Burr look bad. He wrote and spoke against Burr, calling him corrupt and ambitious. He said Burr would "disturb our institutions to secure to himself permanent power." He told anyone who would listen that Burr was immoral—all to wreck his reputation and ruin his chances for success.

And what did Burr say about Hamilton? No record exists of Burr ever saying anything critical of his rival. He did, however, demand apologies from Hamilton on two occasions when Hamilton went too far. Both times, Hamilton apologized.

Then, in 1804, Burr ran for governor of New York and lost. Hamilton had campaigned on behalf of Burr's opponent. After the election, Burr learned that Hamilton had called him "despicable," which at that time was a deep personal insult. Perhaps Hamilton's insult had affected the election. Even if it hadn't, Burr demanded that he take it back. When Hamilton refused, the duel was set.

CHEATER FOR THE PRESIDENCY?

The United States has seen plenty of nasty presidential elections. But the election of 1800 might have been the most controversial. It was infused with hateful insults, harsh accusations, and fierce partisanship. That might sound a lot like recent presidential elections. But what makes the 1800 election unique is how it was resolved.

Back then, citizens didn't vote directly for president. State legislators chose electors, and electors voted for two candidates for president. Whoever got the most votes became president. The runner-up became vice president. In the previous presidential election, in 1796, Federalist John Adams defeated Thomas Jefferson, who was a Democratic-Republican.

Aaron Burr and his fellow Democratic-Republicans didn't want that to happen again. So Burr organized the party. He traveled the country and talked to electors about their votes. He even invited them to his home for meals. In the end, Jefferson and Burr solidified Democratic-Republican electors and were chosen as presidential candidates for that party. The idea was that Jefferson would be president and Burr would be vice president.

Instead, the voting ended in a tie between Jefferson and Burr. That meant the House of Representatives had to vote to decide the presidential election. Each state got one vote. The winner needed a majority of states to win—which at that time was nine states. The Federalists, who hated Jefferson, held enough states to keep his total at eight. If some states voted for Burr, they could prevent Jefferson, or anyone, from getting the nine votes needed. If nobody got nine votes, nobody would win. For them, it was better to have no president at all than to have a Democratic-Republican in office.

As for Burr, he stated that Jefferson should be president. In resolving the tie, he wrote that there should be "no indecency, no unfairness, no personal abuse." He didn't intend to unfairly make a grab for the presidency. And he didn't think anyone else should, either.

The Constitution offered no solution to the deadlock. Things quickly got weird. Democratic-Republicans and Federalists tried to figure out how to get the votes they

By Yesterday's Mails.

Highly Important and Interesting.

PENNSYLVANIA.   PHILAD. FEB. 14.
BY EXPRESS.
WASHINGTON, Feb. 11, half past 3, afternoon.

For THOMAS JEFFERSON, 73
AARON BURR, 73
JOHN ADAMS, 65
C. C. PINCKNEY, 64
JOHN JAY, 1

Congress of the United States.

HOUSE OF REPRESENTATIVES.
FRIDAY, FEB. 6, 1801.

On February 14, 1801, the *Columbian Centinel* of Boston reported "Election Deadlock, 1800."

needed. They wrote letters, made speeches, and held secret meetings to try to influence the Representatives' votes. The Federalists made plans to run the nation through other branches, which they controlled. They smeared Jefferson, and many Federalists actually came around to liking Burr.

It was at this time that Alexander Hamilton became alarmed. Like other Federalists, he hated Jefferson. But Hamilton hated Burr even more. He launched an anti-Burr campaign. Hamilton wrote letters to Federalists all over the country demonizing Burr. He said Burr was unbalanced and immoral. He compared Burr to an ancient Roman traitor named Cataline, who murdered his own family. Burr, he said, was selfish, narcissistic, eager for war, and utterly corrupt. And, according to Hamilton, Burr was broke and planned to use the presidency to make himself rich and powerful. None of this was true. But because Hamilton was a well-respected politician, many people believed him.

Members of both parties got more and more concerned. The nation was young. Peaceful transition of power was rare in the world. People worried that if no president was peacefully selected, someone might try to seize power in a non-peaceful way. Writers predicted coups, assassinations, arson, and more. Some states threatened to leave the union if they didn't get their way.

The longer this went on, the more Hamilton's words about Burr had an effect. Some people believed he was secretly working with both parties to seize the presidency from Jefferson. In truth, Burr wanted to honor the original plan his own party had made. Jefferson should be president, and he should be vice president. Jefferson himself wrote that Burr's "conduct has been honorable and decisive."

In the end, the representative from Delaware, a Federalist state, agreed to vote for Jefferson. Aaron Burr became vice president and never tried to steal the presidency. But Hamilton's letters and papers became important historical documents. Historians looked back on this election through his words—and his words about Burr described a power-hungry, double-dealing tyrant in the making.

TRAITOR AGAINST HIS COUNTRY?

In 1800, Aaron Burr's career was at its height. He had been an officer in the Continental Army, a successful lawyer, a New York assemblyman, and a U.S. senator. Now he was vice president of the United States. But over the next four years, his fortunes changed drastically. He shot and killed Alexander Hamilton and faced possible murder charges. Thomas Jefferson had grown to distrust him and dropped him as his vice president in 1805. Burr then ran for governor of New York and lost. Neither political party wanted anything to do with him. His career was in ruins.

It would seem that things couldn't get much worse for Burr. But in the summer of 1807, he was on trial for treason, one of the most severe crimes anyone can commit against his nation. Jefferson and others believed that he had planned to take over U.S. territory in the western frontier and establish an independent nation. Burr was accused of trying to be emperor of this new nation.

Could this be true? It didn't seem like the actions of a politician who had highly valued fairness and cooperation. Nor did it sound like the city-dwelling man who had no experience living in rough land.

This mysterious story starts in 1804, when Burr began planning a great military adventure into the American frontier. Nobody knows for sure what he was up to. One version of the story says that he was interested in conquering the Spanish-held territory of Mexico. Burr planned a filibuster. At that time a filibuster was an invasion into enemy territory by a private army that was not supported by the government. Filibusters were illegal, but there was an important exception to that law. During times of war, they were legal. Burr believed that the United States would soon be at war with Spain. He would use that opportunity to invade Mexico, claiming the lands for the United States. He would be a hero!

Early in 1805, Burr and a small army traveled along the Ohio and Mississippi Rivers for several months. They were scouting territory and recruiting supporters. When he returned east, Burr found that people were talking about him. What was he doing with all those volunteers out west? Perhaps he was planning a revolution against the United States.

The following summer, Burr went back out west to gather his troops to prepare for his filibuster. But while he was gone, one of Burr's allies betrayed him. General James Wilkinson was the highest-ranking officer in the

Aaron Burr encouraged his followers on their expedition into the western frontier at Blennerhassett Island in the Ohio River in 1805.

U.S. Army and had been helping Burr. But he changed his mind and told Jefferson that Burr was up to some conspiracy out west. A furious Jefferson issued an order for Burr's arrest.

Burr was captured in February 1807 near present-day Mobile, Alabama. He was returned to Virginia to face trial.

Aaron Burr's trial for treason was called the trial of the century.

To this day, it's not clear exactly what his plan was. What we do know is that Jefferson insisted that he be tried for treason, which was punishable by death.

The trial began that summer. Wilkinson produced a letter he said was written by Burr. The letter, he said, was a coded message that proved Burr's treasonous plans. However, Burr and his lawyers proved that Wilkinson had forged the letter. They also argued that there was not enough evidence against Burr. The Constitution requires an "overt act" by the accused. But prosecutors could not prove one. The jury found Burr not guilty of treason.

Burr was free to go, but his reputation was further damaged. He had been one of the nation's founding fathers and a defender of its core values. Now he was one of the most hated men in America.

FATHER OF MARTIN VAN BUREN?

After his treason trial, Burr fled to Europe. When he returned to New York in 1812, he was struggling financially. He asked the New York legislature for a land grant. The land would be payment for his time in the military. He argued that he had served four years in the army in New York. His health had suffered from the war. For that reason, it was hard for him to make a living. He should receive a pension for his service. Other veterans were making similar appeals to the national Congress.

Burr got help with his appeal from several people. One was a New York legislator named Martin Van Buren. In 1804, Van Buren had supported Burr's opponent when he ran for governor. But any previous animosity was now behind them. The two were becoming close friends. They were also tied together by a rumor that Van Buren was the illegitimate son of Burr.

Martin Van Buren

The two men did look somewhat alike. They were both short and dressed sharply. They even both grew large sideburns. What's more, they shared similar views of the law and government. Over the years, they would collaborate on many cases together as lawyers. Van Buren was 26 years younger than Burr. But was Burr his father?

With his first wife, Burr had only one child. His daughter, Theodosia, died at sea in 1812 or 1813 when her ship was lost or raided by pirates. But he helped raise several children throughout his life. His wife had five children from her previous marriage. Burr raised the two youngest boys as his own. He provided for their education and helped them launch their careers.

Burr was also known to have relationships with many women. It is almost certain that he had children out of wedlock. After he returned from Europe, he cared for several children. He was probably the natural father of some of them.

Burr seems to have been a kind and generous father to some, and a father figure to others. But Martin Van Buren was not his child. Van Buren's father was Abraham Van Buren, a patriot of the American Revolution and an inn and tavern owner. There has never been any evidence that Burr and Martin Van Buren were related.

Burr never did get a pension from the state of New York. Later, he shifted his focus to the federal Congress. But in a letter to his friend Van Buren, he said, "I have no prospects of growing richer or younger."

By then Van Buren was the vice president of the United States. He was in a better position to do something for his older friend. Van Buren helped push Burr's claim through. In 1834, Burr finally received his compensation from the government. He died two years later.

CHAPTER THREE
THE LESSER-KNOWN BURR

*M*any people know the story of Aaron Burr's duel with Alexander Hamilton. They may know he was an early senator and vice president. But some of his lesser-known accomplishments changed U.S. history and still affect us today.

MONOPOLY BUSTER

Burr spent the 1780s and 1790s living in New York City. He practiced law, and he entered politics. There were two major parties in New York politics at that time. They were the Federalists and the Democratic-Republicans. Burr was a Democratic-Republican. His rival, Alexander Hamilton, was a Federalist.

The Federalists favored a strong central government, and they controlled the New York state government.

Alexander Hamilton and Philip Schuyler meet Aaron Burr and his daughter as they walk along Wall Street in New York City.

They also controlled all the banks in New York City. This practice is what is known as a monopoly. They wouldn't allow Democratic-Republicans to open their own banks. They wouldn't lend money to them either.

Burr was determined to change this. In 1798, he got his chance. There was a serious health crisis in New York City. Yellow fever was spreading quickly, and people were dying. They needed access to clean drinking water to control the epidemic. Burr decided to start a private business that would provide fresh, clean water to New Yorkers.

Burr needed the permission of the state government to open the water business. So he wrote a charter describing the business and how it would work. He called it the Manhattan Company. He described how it would help improve the lives of New Yorkers. He even got his Federalist rival, Alexander Hamilton, to support his plan.

The State Assembly voted to allow him to start the business as described in the charter. But Burr had done something sneaky in the document. He had included wording that said the business could use any extra profits for other purposes. They just couldn't break the law.

The "other purposes" that Burr had in mind was just one—banking. In fact, he planned to have banking be the main focus of his new company. He would loan money to Democratic-Republicans who couldn't borrow from other banks. And he would earn interest on the loans. The Manhattan Company didn't deliver much water at all. But it has since become J.P. Morgan, one of the world's largest banks.

CHAMPION OF TENNESSEE

By 1806, Aaron Burr's reputation had crumbled. So had his influence on national politics. Thomas Jefferson had booted him from the position of vice president. He had shot and killed Alexander Hamilton. And he had lost an election for governor of New York. So he spent some time out west, including in the new state of Tennessee. That was one place where he was still welcomed and much loved. At one point he stayed at the home of Andrew Jackson, the future U.S. president. Jackson even tried to convince Burr to move to his state and run for public office. He would easily win, Jackson said.

Why was Burr so popular in Tennessee at the same time he was despised in most of the rest of the country? Burr played an important role in getting Tennessee admitted to the Union as a state.

In the 1790s, the area that is now Tennessee was a U.S. territory. The government wanted people to settle the area, so a road was built from North Carolina. But neither the government of North Carolina nor that of the United States provided much further assistance.

Migrating to the western frontier at that time was difficult and dangerous. So was living there once you arrived. Settlers leaving the relative comfort of eastern cities would need more than a road. Residents in the area believed they would receive more support if Tennessee were a state. So in 1796, Tennessee officials applied for statehood.

But they did not foresee the challenge their request would face. The challenge arose because of politics. Admission to the Union would give Tennessee citizens the right to vote in national elections. Federalists in U.S. government believed that Tennessee would vote for Democratic-Republicans. This could tip the balance of power so that someone like Thomas Jefferson could be elected president. That idea disgusted Federalists, so they fiercely opposed statehood for Tennessee.

Both houses of Congress had to approve the measure, starting with the House of Representatives. When the issue came up for a vote, Federalist congressmen spoke against it. But the Democratic-Republicans held a majority in the House, so the measure passed.

The Senate, however, was controlled by Federalists. They didn't even bring the bill up for a vote. The House urged them to reconsider. Finally, the two houses of Congress created a joint committee to discuss the issue. Senator Aaron Burr of New York was one of the committee's managers. Historians say that it was Burr who finally persuaded the committee to recommend admitting Tennessee. On his recommendation, the bill was voted on in the Senate and passed.

A map of the U.S. during the election of 1800 shows that Thomas Jefferson received 73 electoral votes, and John Adams got 65. Tennessee voted for Jefferson.

DEMOCRATIC.—THOS. JEFFERSON of Va., received 73 votes.
FEDERALIST.—JOHN ADAMS of Mass., received 65 votes.
A tie occuring between Jefferson, and Burr the Democratic Candidate for Vice-President, throws the election into the House, which balloted from Feb. 11th to the 17th, finally electing Jefferson on the 36th ballot.
AARON BURR of New York became Vice-President.
Jefferson was born in 1743, in the British Colony of Virginia, he was of Welsh descent, and was a lawyer, educated at College. Was author of the "Declaration of Independence." Died July 4, 1826.

On June 1, 1796, Tennessee officially became the 16th U.S. state. Aaron Burr became forever beloved there. William Blount, one the state's first senators, summed up Tennesseans' feelings. He wrote, "I pronounce positively that Mr. Burr . . . may be ranked among [Tennessee's] warmest friends."

Tennessee did vote for Jefferson for president in 1800, along with Burr for vice president. And later, after Jefferson had dropped Burr, Tennessee's politicians remained among Burr's only loyal supporters.

KEEPING HAMILTON OUT OF A DUEL

Aaron Burr and Alexander Hamilton faced each other in the most famous duel in U.S. history. When Burr shot Hamilton in 1804, he became a notorious villain. Throughout history, it has been the one thing he is most known for. But 12 years earlier, Burr and Hamilton were nearly involved in another duel together. That time, no one was killed.

Like most stories involving these two men, it all started with politics and gossip. In 1792, the Democratic-Republicans wanted to remove Federalist John Adams from his position of vice president. The man they wanted to run in his place was Aaron Burr.

Hamilton was already fiercely opposed to Burr. Burr was a rising talent and a major threat to the Federalists. Hamilton campaigned against him, mainly by writing letters to influential politicians. His criticisms of Burr were basically the same as those he would make in the presidential election years later. He said Burr had no principles. He said Burr was poor with finances. And he said Burr was power-hungry. Burr was so detestable, according to Hamilton, that he said he had "a religious duty to oppose [Burr's] career."

To defend Burr, some Democratic-Republicans began to do research into Hamilton's own life. One of them was Senator James Monroe. Monroe discovered that Hamilton might have been engaged in illegal activity against the government. A man named James Reynolds claimed that he was involved in a scheme with Hamilton. He said Hamilton had used his position as U.S. Treasury Secretary to take government funds.

James Monroe

When Monroe confronted Hamilton, Hamilton admitted that he had done something wrong. But it was not what Reynolds claimed. Rather, Hamilton was having an affair with Maria Reynolds, James Reynolds's wife. Hamilton didn't want people to find out he was involved with a woman who was not his wife. If they did, his political career would be severely damaged. So Reynolds blackmailed Hamilton to keep the affair secret.

Monroe agreed to keep Hamilton's secret. But five years later, a journalist discovered the affair and wrote about it. Hamilton was certain that Monroe had broken his promise and leaked the story. He confronted Monroe, whose friend David Gelston wrote down the conversation.

Monroe insisted he hadn't leaked the story, but Hamilton didn't believe him. "Do you say I represented falsely," Monroe said. "You are a Scoundrel."

"I will meet you like a Gentleman," Hamilton replied. That meant he wanted a duel.

"I am ready," Monroe responded. "Get your pistols."

Monroe's friend broke up the fight, but the men continued arguing for weeks. Neither man thought it was honorable to back down. And both accused the other of being a coward. A duel was planned and seemed inevitable until Aaron Burr intervened. Monroe chose him as his "second," or his assistant. Burr thought the two men were being childish and told them so. Eventually, he convinced them to let the issue go.

Burr's actions may have saved Hamilton's life that day. Seven years later, he would take it himself.

CHAPTER FOUR
A DARKER SIDE

Aaron Burr's allies knew him as thoughtful and fair. Modern supporters see him as enlightened and principled. But he definitely had a bad reputation during his lifetime. To get a fuller picture of Burr, it's important to look at some of the darker truths about him.

KILLER OF ALEXANDER HAMILTON

The long-bubbling feud between Alexander Hamilton and Aaron Burr came to its conclusion in the summer of 1804. The two men had very different ideas about politics and government. They also had different thoughts about public conflict. For years Hamilton had publicly criticized Burr. He'd spread rumors, often without regard to the truth. He had called Burr terrible names. Burr, by contrast, preferred to let his reputation speak for itself.

He didn't engage in gossip or personal attacks. He even taught his daughter, Theodosia, when she was 13, to do the same. "Receive with calmness every reproof," he said, "whether made kindly or unkindly; whether just or unjust."

But in 1804, Hamilton finally said something that pushed Burr to fight back. Early that year, Burr had run for governor of New York. As usual, Hamilton campaigned against him. After Burr lost, a letter was published in the *Albany Register*, a New York newspaper. It was written by Dr. Charles D. Cooper, who had heard Hamilton speak against Burr during the campaign. According to Cooper, Hamilton said many things about Burr. But one insult in particular angered Burr.

Cooper wrote, "I could detail to you a still more despicable opinion which General Hamilton has expressed of Mr. Burr."

The word "despicable" meant that Hamilton thought Burr had engaged in unacceptable or sleazy behavior. It was a deeply personal and harsh insult about Burr's private character. He wrote to Hamilton and asked him to retract the statement. Twice before, in their 15-year history of public battles, he had done the same thing. And twice before, Hamilton had apologized for his offending remark. Burr had accepted the apologies and forgiven Hamilton. This time, however, Hamilton would not apologize. After a series of angry letters between the two men, a duel was set.

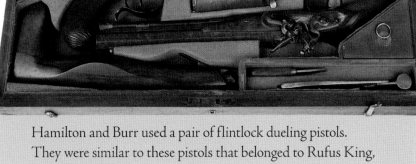

Hamilton and Burr used a pair of flintlock dueling pistols.
They were similar to these pistols that belonged to Rufus King,
a signer of Declaration of Independence and a United States
senator from New York.

On July 11, the two men met on the west bank of the
Hudson River. The site was the Weehawken dueling
ground in New Jersey. Because Burr had issued the
challenge, Hamilton got to supply the weapons. He
provided two pistols equipped with hair triggers, which
made their shots unpredictable. He supplied one-ounce
balls—a deadly bullet.

Both men had written letters to settle their affairs in
the event that they died. In his letter, Hamilton wrote
that he did not intend to fire at Burr with his first shot.

He hoped that by holding back, Burr would reconsider the matter. But witnesses to the scene say that before the contest, Hamilton tested his aim. He pointed the gun from different positions and in different areas of sunlight. He did all this to improve his accuracy. They believed he intended to fire.

Burr (left) and Hamilton (right) met at the dueling grounds near Weehawken, New Jersey, at 7:00 am on July 11, 1804.

Indeed, one of the witnesses reported that, when the word was given to fire, Hamilton shot first. Burr was not hit, and he returned fire. His ball struck Hamilton, who died the next day. That shot did what all of Hamilton's smears could not quite accomplish. It made Burr one of the biggest villains in U.S. history.

DYING DESPISED, HEARTBROKEN, AND BROKE

After Burr had killed Hamilton and been accused of treason, his life was in shambles. When Burr was found not guilty of treason in October 1807, he was free to get on with his life. But it wasn't easy. For one thing, he had huge debts. He had borrowed large sums for land speculation deals that had gone bad. He owed about $36,000—more than $780,000 in today's dollars.

But he had an even bigger problem—people hated him. His name had become a synonym for traitor. When he traveled from the court in Virginia, he passed through Baltimore. The mayor there provided an armed escort to protect him from being killed by angry citizens.

Burr made it safely to New York. But he often had to use a false name as he traveled. He had one particularly powerful enemy in President Thomas Jefferson. Jefferson still did not trust Burr. He told others that he believed Burr was actively trying to find a way to damage the country.

Burr realized that his reputation would make it impossible to achieve success in the United States. He decided to move to Europe. There, he felt, he could prove himself once again. He could also make money to pay off his debts.

But travel was still difficult for him. His many enemies were afraid he would try to go to another country to conspire against the United States. So Burr hatched a plan with his adult daughter to disguise his travels.

First, his daughter told the newspapers that her father was traveling by land to Canada. Then, under a false name, Burr sailed to England. He arrived in London in 1808.

Burr traveled through Europe for more than two years, poor but getting by. Finally he boarded a ship sailing for the United States. Burr was very nervous about returning home. He feared being rejected for his past actions—and harassed by his creditors.

He finally arrived in Manhattan in the summer of 1812, his identity hidden. He opened a law practice, ready to rebuild his life. Sadly, that same month Burr received a letter from his daughter in South Carolina. Her son, Burr's only grandson, had died at age 11. Theodosia's husband was commanding the South Carolina militia in the War of 1812 against Great Britain. So she set sail for New York to be with her father during this sad time.

Theodosia never made it. Tragedy struck Burr again, as his daughter's ship was lost at sea. Heartbroken and still penniless, he lived out his years in New York City practicing law.

Burr had one last chance to find happiness and financial relief when he met a wealthy widow named Eliza Jumel. He married her in 1833. Burr was 77 years old, and Jumel was 58. However, Jumel filed for divorce less than two years later.

During the long court proceedings, Burr suffered a major stroke. The divorce became final on September 14, 1836. Burr died that same day.

Burr died at the age of 80. He is buried in Princeton, New Jersey.

A CHANGING LEGACY

In 1807, the same year that Aaron Burr was facing charges of treason in Virginia, an anonymous Federalist published his "Portrait of Burr." This document criticized Burr in ways that, by then, were familiar. Burr was "mysterious." He was empty of any real convictions—all show and no substance.

Critiques like this may seem mild to our modern eyes. But at the time, they were cutting. To be shallow was a harsh assessment of a man. And the insults in "Portrait of Burr" summed up what Burr had faced his whole life. They were jabs he would continue to face even after his death. His legacy as a villain would live on for generations, even into modern times.

But the truth of Aaron Burr is more complicated. He certainly had bad luck during his lifetime. Some of his worst luck was to earn the distrust of powerful men such as Thomas Jefferson and Alexander Hamilton. Historians now agree that there are two sides to the stories involving Jefferson, Hamilton, and Burr. Unfortunately for Burr, this era of history was written largely in the voices of Jefferson and Hamilton. Both men had many letters and other writings that survived them. Meanwhile, most of Burr's personal writings were lost in a shipwreck. His wife and daughter died before him, and he had nobody to defend his legacy. In short, he didn't get a chance to tell his side of the story.

Nevertheless, more historians are beginning to see Burr in a positive light. Most agree that his sense of democracy and fairness was among the best of the founding fathers. He consistently fought for the rights of common people. As a state senator, he tried to end slavery and allow women to vote. These two ideas were way ahead of their time.

Later, as a U.S. senator, Burr was known for his independent thinking. Unlike many politicians, he did not ally himself too closely with either political party—or with the wealthy establishment. He fought to help veterans and those widowed or orphaned by the war. He supported the rights of working people in allowing them to own land and vote.

Of course, a huge part of Burr's reputation has been defined by one deed—killing Alexander Hamilton. But even here, modern historians are coming down more on Burr's side. Yes, he shot Hamilton. But evidence suggested that he had been bullied by Hamilton for decades. And it took two people to duel. Burr is certainly responsible for Hamilton's death. But he may not be the villain he has often been portrayed to be.

TIMELINE

1756
Aaron Burr is born in Newark, New Jersey, on February 6.

1757
Burr's father dies.

1758
Burr's mother dies.

1772
Burr graduates from the College of New Jersey,
later known as Princeton University.

1775
Burr joins a military attack on Quebec.

1776
Burr leads a successful retreat from Manhattan
after the British invade it.

1777
Burr is promoted to lieutenant colonel.

1778
In poor health, Burr takes leave from the military in October.

1782
Burr is admitted to the New York state bar
and marries Theodosia Prevost Bartow.

1783
Burr's daughter, Theodosia, is born.

1784-1785
Burr serves in the New York State Assembly.

1789-1790
Burr serves as attorney general of New York State.

1791
Burr defeats Philip Schuyler for a seat in the U.S. Senate.

1794
Burr's wife, Theodosia, dies.

1801
Burr becomes vice president.

1804
Burr kills Alexander Hamilton in a duel.

1805
Burr begins exploring land on the frontier

1806
Jefferson calls for Burr to be arrested for treason.

1807
Burr goes on trial for treason and is found not guilty.

1808
Burr sails to England under a false identity.

1812
Burr returns to the United States under a false identity.
He moves to New York and opens a law office.
Burr's daughter, Theodosia, is lost at sea.

1830
Burr suffers a stroke.

1833
Burr marries Eliza Jumel.

1834
Burr suffers another stroke. Jumel files for divorce.

1836
Burr dies September 14, the same day his divorce is finalized.

GLOSSARY

animosity—a strong dislike for someone

corrupt—willing to break laws to get money or power

Democratic-Republican—an early American political party that favored restricting the powers of the national government and increasing states' rights

Federalist—an early American political party that favored a strong central government and supported the U.S. Constitution

feminist—someone who believes strongly that women ought to have the same opportunities and rights that men have

filibuster—an invasion into enemy territory by a private army that is not supported by the government

forge—to falsely make or alter a writing

illegitimate—describes a child born to parents who aren't married

monopoly—a situation in which there is only one supplier of a good or service, and therefore that supplier can control the price

pension—money paid regularly to a retired person

Tory—a member of a political party that supported the British government during the American Revolution

traitor—someone who aids the enemy of his of her country

treason—the crime of betraying your country

FURTHER READING

Gunderson, Jessica. *The Real Alexander Hamilton: The Truth Behind the Legend*. North Mankato, MN: Capstone Press, 2019.

McGrath, Brian. *Aaron Burr: More Than a Villain*. Huntington Beach, CA: Teacher Created Materials Library, 2017.

Worth, Richard. *Alexander Hamilton and Aaron Burr*. New York: Enslow, 2018.

INTERNET SITES

Aaron Burr
www.biography.com/people/aaron-burr-9232241

Aaron Burr
www.history.com/tag/aaron-burr

The Burr Conspiracy
www.pbs.org/wgbh/americanexperience/features/duel-burr-conspiracy

SOURCE NOTES

Page 15, "work of genius" Nancy Isenberg. *Fallen Founder: The Life of Aaron Burr*. New York: Penguin Books, 2008, p. 83.

Page 15, "Is it owing to ignorance..." Ibid., p.83.

Page 15, "women have souls" Ibid., p. 83.

Page 25, "dirty earwig" Ibid., p. 46.

Page 26, "disturb our institutions..." David O. Stewart. *American Emperor: Aaron Burr's Challenge to Jefferson's America*. New York: Simon & Schuster, 2011, p. 21.

Page 27, "despicable" Ibid., p. 30.

Page 28, "no indecency..." *Fallen Founder: The Life of Aaron Burr*, p. 208.

Page 31, "conduct has been honorable..." Ibid., p. 218.

Page 37, "I have no prospects..." Ibid., p. 399.

Page 43, "I pronounce positively..." James Parton. *Life of Andrew Jackson: In Three Volumes*. New York: Mason Brothers, 1860, p. 201.

Page 44, "a religious duty..." *Fallen Founder: The Life of Aaron Burr*, p. 119.

Page 45, "Do you say I represented falsely..." Cassandra Good, "That Time When Alexander Hamilton Almost Dueled James Monroe," Smithsonian.com, October 26, 2015, www.smithsonianmag.com/history/time-when-alexander-hamilton-almost-dueled-james-monroe-180957045/, Accessed March 21, 2019.

Page 48, "Receive with calmness..." *Fallen Founder: The Life of Aaron Burr*, p. 165.

Page 48, "I could detail to you..." Ibid., p. 257.

SELECT BIBLIOGRAPHY

Good, Cassandra, "That Time When Alexander Hamilton Almost Dueled James Monroe," Smithsonian.com, October 26, 2015.

Isenberg, Nancy. *Fallen Founder: The Life of Aaron Burr*. New York: Penguin Books, 2008.

Parton, James. *Life of Andrew Jackson: In Three Volumes*. New York: Mason Brothers, 1860.

Shearer, Benjamin F. *The United States: Oklahoma to Wyoming*. Westport, CT: Greenwood Publishing Group, 2004.

Stewart, David O. *American Emperor: Aaron Burr's Challenge to Jefferson's America*. New York: Simon & Schuster, 2011.

INDEX